ONCE
UPON A TIME
IN JAPAN
2

KODANSHA INTERNATIONAL
Tokyo • New York • London

ONCE UPON A TIME IN JAPAN

2

Compiled by Sayumi Kawauchi
Translated by Ralph F. McCarthy

Published by Kodansha International Ltd., 17-14,
Otowa 1-chome, Bunkyo-ku, Tokyo 112-8652.

ISBN 4-7700-2213-1

CONTENTS

Baby Grandma

Once upon a time a very old man lived with his wife in a little house way out in the country. They were both so old and feeble that it was all they could do to make it through each day. But they were still very much in love, and by working together and helping each other they managed somehow to get by.

One stormy afternoon, as the old couple sat

before their fireplace, the roof began to leak. *Plip. Plop. Plip, plop, plop.* Raindrops dripped steadily onto the floor beside them.

"You know," said the old man, turning to his wife, "I'd fix that leak if I could, Grandma. But I'm not as young as I used to be."

"Don't worry, Grandpa," replied the gentle old woman. "I don't mind."

And so it went. Life only grew harder for the old couple with each passing day, and they, in turn, became ever more dependent on each other. Both agreed that when the time came they wanted to die together. And they knew it wouldn't be very long now.

But then something happened to change all that. It started one morning when the old man was in the forest gathering firewood and spied some mushrooms.

"Grandma loves mushrooms," he thought. "Long as I'm here, I might as well pick some for her."

So, with his bundle of firewood strapped to his back, the old man shuffled slowly along picking up all the mushrooms he could find. Soon he had gone deeper into the forest than he'd ever been before.

"I guess that ought to be enough," he said to himself when he'd nearly filled his bag. "Now let's see . . . Uh-oh. Which way did I come from?"

The old man was lost. What's more, it was a very hot day, and he was terribly thirsty. Luckily, however, as he was wandering about looking for the path back home, he heard the sound of a waterfall. He followed the sound down a slope, parting the bushes as he went, and came to a little pool.

"Thank goodness," said the old man, kneeling down and putting his hand in the water. "Oh! It's nice and cold, too."

He scooped up a handful and drank. How delicious it tasted! Suddenly he felt better than he had in years. He took another sip, and once again sensed a rush of youthful energy. "Funny," he thought. "I haven't felt like this since I was a kid!"

The old man didn't notice his reflection in the rippling pool. But if he had, he would have been even more surprised. His face was now that of a *young* man. The wrinkles on his

brow were gone, and his white hair had
turned shiny black!

After taking one last drink, the man set out
to look for the path home. This time he found
it easily and headed back toward his house
so full of pep and vitality that he was astonished by the change.

But that was nothing compared to the old
woman's astonishment when her husband
walked through the door.

"I'm home, Grand
ma!" he said. "I'm
sorry it took so
long. I lost my
way."

The old woman

cocked her head. "And who might you be, young fellow?" she asked. "What can I do for you?"

"What are you talking about? It's me."

"It's you, is it? You who?"

"Grandma, have you been napping again? Rub the sleep out of your eyes."

"I'm wide awake, young man. And I've never seen you before in my life."

The man was bewildered. He walked closer to his wife and said, "Grandma, it's me, your husband."

"Now look here, young fellow, if this is some kind of joke . . ." The old woman peered at the man. "Wait a minute," she said. "You're wearing Grandpa's clothes!"

"Of course I am. Why shouldn't I be wearing my own clothes?"

"That voice! That's Grandpa's voice!"

"Of course it's my voice."

"And that face. You look just like Grandpa when he was young!"

"When I was . . . young?" The man turned this over in his mind, remembering how wonderful he'd been feeling since he drank from the mountain pool. Finally, shaking his head, he went to the water barrel to look at his reflection.

"Oh, my!" he exclaimed. "Grandma, what's going on here?"

"Don't ask me!"

The man peered at his face in the water again. "It's me, all right. But how did I get so young? Wait . . . That pool I drank from. It . . . it must have been the fountain of youth!"

The man sat down on the floor with a crash. "Young!" he cried. "Ha, ha! I'm young again!"

Suddenly he stopped laughing, jumped up, and turned to his wife. "But, Grandma," he said, "I don't want to be young all by myself. I'll go get some of that water for you, too." He found a gourd to carry the water in, and was heading out the door when his wife stopped him.

"It's late, Grandpa," she said. "Let's do it tomorrow. That'll give us something to look forward to tonight."

"You don't mind waiting till morning?"

"Heavens, no. If we old people know anything, it's how to be patient."

"Old? Not after tomorrow!"

The youthful Grandpa slept deeply that night. His snores echoed throughout the house. But Grandma was so excited by the thought of becoming young again that she couldn't sleep a wink. Finally she got up and crept quietly out of the house. And by the light of the moon she set off slowly along the path her husband had told her about—the path to the fountain of youth.

At dawn, the man awoke alone. When he saw his wife's futon folded up beside him, he realized she'd gone to look for the pool and chuckled to himself.

"Couldn't wait, eh? I guess she wants to surprise me. All right, Grandma. I'll be right here waiting."

To pass the time until she returned, young Grandpa fixed the leak in the roof and bustled about tending to all the other chores he hadn't been able to do before.

The day wore on but there was no sign of Grandma. By lunchtime, Grandpa began to worry. "Maybe she got lost," he thought.

Finally he decided he couldn't wait any longer. Convinced that something terrible had happened to his wife, he ran up the mountain path as fast as his young legs would carry him. He had almost reached the pool when he heard a noise and stopped.

"What's that?" he wondered. "Sounds like a baby crying."

He pushed on down the slope and through the brush until he came to the edge of the pool. And there he saw his wife's kimono ly-

ing on the ground. "Oh, no!" he cried. "Don't tell me she fell in!" He ran to the kimono and was about to pick it up when he jumped back with a gasp. Inside was a little baby girl!

"G-Grandma?" whispered the man.

That's right. The old woman had been so eager to surprise her husband that she had drunk much more of the water than she needed. And the fountain of youth had done its work only too well. It had turned her into an infant.

The man picked his tiny wife up in his arms and carried her home. And from that day on, they say, he was as busy as a man can be, changing diapers, washing, cooking, and cleaning up after Baby Grandma.

Hachisuke and the White Fox

One day long, long ago, the Lord of
Obama was strolling through the
streets of his town. At that time
Obama was a fast-growing, bustling seaport.
The kindhearted lord, whose castle was in the
center of town, often took a leisurely walk
after lunch to mix with the local people.

On this particular day he was making his
way back to the castle when he heard a sud-
den great yipping and yapping. A moment
later a snow-white fox came skidding around
a corner. And right
behind it were four very
angry men.

"We've got you now,
you little thief!" yelled

one of the men. He pounced on the animal and started to hit and kick it as hard as he could. The little fox yelped and howled in pain.

"You there," the Lord of Obama called out, approaching the men. "Don't you think that's enough? Look at the poor thing—you've nearly killed him."

"But, your lordship," said the man still holding the fox, "you should see what he did to our store. He kicked everything over and chewed up our dried fish. What a mess!"

"He did, did he? I see. All right then, I'll tell you what. I'll pay for the damage, but I want you to hand that fox over to me."

The men, of course, agreed, and the kind-hearted lord carried the fox back to his castle. He told his servants to spare no expense in caring for the animal and to prepare lots of fried tofu, which is a great favorite of foxes. With this kind treatment, the fox got better in no time. Within a few days, in fact, he was as healthy and frisky as ever. And so one evening when he'd completely recovered,

the Lord of Obama took him to the foot of a mountain just outside town.

"Now listen, little one," he said as he let the fox go. "You're not to be coming back and stealing things from people. Understand? All right, then. Go on home now."

The fox trotted hesitantly up the moonlit mountain path, stopping time and again to turn and gaze back toward the castle of the kindhearted lord.

Obama was never troubled with mischievous foxes again, and the town continued to grow and prosper as the months went by. But then came the fateful day when the Lord of Obama thought he had lost it all. He had to see to it that a certain message was delivered to Edo, the capital, within seven days. If the message didn't get to Edo in time, the lord and his family would be disgraced and ruined. But the lord's messenger—a man named Goheiji—had suddenly fallen ill and wouldn't be able to make the long journey. The Lord of Obama was at his wit's end.

"Oh, no. Who else can get to Edo in a week?" he moaned. "Isn't there anyone else?"

As a matter of fact, there wasn't. No one in Obama could run nearly as fast as Goheiji. But just as the lord was about to give up hope, a stranger arrived at the castle gates. When he was brought before the lord, he bowed deeply and introduced himself.

"My name is Hachisuke," he said. "I was passing through your town when I heard of your lordship's need for a swift messenger. If I can be of any assistance . . ."

"Are you fast?"

"Quite."

"Ah, but I don't suppose you can get to Edo in seven days, can you?" sighed the lord.

"I can."

The lord hesitated. After all, he'd never

even seen this man before. But the fellow certainly seemed confident enough . . .

"All right, Hachisuke," he said finally, slapping his knee. "You're hired. I'm depending on you, my boy."

The box containing the vital letter was brought, and the next moment Hachisuke was off and running.

Seven days later, the Lord of Obama sat in his office counting on his fingers. He had hardly slept all week. "One, two, three, four, five, six, seven. So it's been a week today," he muttered. "Let's just hope Hachisuke reaches Edo by this afternoon . . ."

No sooner had he said this than a servant rushed excitedly into the room. "Your lordship!" he cried. "Hachisuke has returned!"

"Returned? Oh, no!" The lord buried his face in his hands. "I might have known he'd never make it. Well, it's all over now. I'm a ruined man."

"You misunderstand me, your lord-

ship," said the servant. "Hachisuke has been to Edo and back. And he's waiting outside now with the reply to your letter!"

"What? That's impossible!"

Hachisuke was summoned. He fell to his knees before the lord and presented him with the letter from Edo. The lord was as delighted as he was flabbergasted.

"There's no doubt about it. This is the official reply from Edo. My family is saved! Hachisuke, how can I ever repay you?"

"To be of service to your lordship," replied the messenger, "is all I desire."

"But how did you do it, my boy? Not even Goheiji can make it to Edo and back in less than two weeks!"

Hachisuke only smiled and bowed even lower.

From that day on, Hachisuke became the castle's most trusted messenger. During the months that followed he made any number of trips to Edo and back. One evening he had just returned from a mission when the lord called for him and said, "Well done, lad. Now rest easy for a few days."

"Thank you, your lordship."

"By the way, Hachisuke, I've been wondering . . . What's the most difficult part of the trip to Edo?"

"There's no difficulty to speak of, your lordship," replied Hachisuke. "Except . . ."

"Yes?"

"Except, perhaps, for the wild dogs near Odawara . . ."

"Dogs? Ha, ha! A man like you, Hachisuke, afraid of dogs? Surely you're joking. Ha, ha, ha!"

Hachisuke blushed and scratched his head in embarrassment.

Several days later the messenger set off for the capital with another letter. But though he promised to be back within ten days, two weeks went by and still there was no sign of him.

Well into the third week, the Lord of Obama started to get worried. What if Hachisuke had met with some terrible accident? he thought with a shudder. It was only then that he remembered what the trusty messenger had said about the wild dogs near Odawara.

"Good heavens! Could it be . . . ?" The lord immediately summoned his servants and ordered them to saddle some horses. As soon as this was done, he set out with them toward Odawara to look for Hachisuke.

They searched for several days with no luck. It was on their way home, in the mountains between Odawara and Obama, that the lord pointed at something in the weeds beside the road.

"What's that?" he said.

The servants could see a white object lying among the weeds. One of them got off his horse and went to investigate.

"Your lordship!" he shouted a moment later. "It's the letter box!"

"Any trace of Hachisuke?" the lord called out, dismounting and hurrying to the spot. When he got there, however, he turned ghostly pale and fell, trembling, to his knees. "Good heavens!" he gasped. "The white fox!"

The limp, lifeless body of a small white fox was draped over the letter box as if to protect it. Everything was clear to the lord now. He took the dead animal in his arms and

sobbed. "Hachisuke!" he cried. "Hachisuke!"

Yes, Hachisuke and the white fox were one and the same. To repay the Lord of Obama for his kindness, the fox had transformed himself into the fleet-footed messenger. Tracked down and savagely attacked by the wild dogs, he had died of his wounds as he struggled to make it back to the castle.

Obama Castle no longer stands. But where the castle grounds used to be there remains a shrine that was built by the kindhearted lord. The shrine is named after the faithful Hachisuke, and it's dedicated to Inari, the fox-deity, who looks out for messengers everywhere.

Princess Flowerpot

Once upon a time, in the countryside near Osaka, there lived a very beautiful and sweet-natured little girl. Growing up on her father's big estate, she had always been a carefree, playful, and happy child. Recently, however, her days were filled with sadness and worry. Her mother, whom she loved more than anyone in the world, had suddenly become very, very sick.

One night the little girl went to her mother's bedside and said, "Mama, when are you going to get better?"

"You mustn't worry about me," replied the gentle lady. "I may have to leave you soon. But I'll be going to a wonderful place. And someday we'll be together again . . ."

"But I don't want you to go, Mama!"

The lady's eyes filled with tears. Who will look after my little girl when I'm gone? she thought. Later, as she lay in bed unable to sleep, she decided to ask Kannon, the Goddess of Mercy, for help. "Kannon," she prayed, "I'm not afraid to die. But if I do, what will become of my little girl? How can I be certain no harm will come to her?"

She prayed on and on until at last, well past midnight, she fell asleep. And as soon as she did so, the goddess appeared to her in a dream.

"If you want your daughter to be safe and happy," Kannon said, "cover her head with a flowerpot."

Cover her head with a flowerpot? It was an unusual piece of advice, to say the least. But the mother didn't doubt the wisdom of the goddess's words for a moment. When she awoke she found a large flowerpot, placed it over her daughter's head, and prayed once again for the child's happiness.

It was only a few days later when the dying woman called for her little girl and whispered weakly, "The time has come for me to go to heaven, dear. Never forget how your mother loves you."

"Mama!" cried the little girl. "Please don't leave me alone!"

But in the next instant her mother was gone.

How lonely the girl was from that day on! Her father was so busy that she rarely even saw him. Only once in the weeks following the funeral did he come to his daughter's room. And then it was only to say, "Let's take off that silly pot, shall we?" Pull as he might, however, the flowerpot wouldn't come off. He called for his servants, but none of them could loosen it either. It was stuck fast to the little girl's head.

And that's the way it stayed. Before long everyone became used to it, and even her father took to calling her "Flowerpot"—when he bothered to speak to her, that is.

One day he came home with a lady the girl had never seen before. "Flowerpot," he said, "this is your new mother. You are to honor and obey her. Is that clear?"

Flowerpot nodded and bowed. But the lady simply shook her head and scowled. "Disgusting little creature," she hissed. "What is that ridiculous thing on her head?"

That wasn't a very good start. And as time went by, Flowerpot's cold-hearted stepmother only came to despise her more. Finally, on a freezing winter's day some months later, she summoned her servants. "I want you to get rid of that horrid little girl," she told them. "Take her somewhere far, far away. And don't bring her back!"

Poor Flowerpot! That very day she was left all by herself in a snowy wilderness miles and

miles from home. From then on she had to wander through the countryside, penniless and alone. And having that pot stuck to her head didn't help. Wherever she went, mean little children teased her and older people pointed and laughed.

"Ha, ha! What's

that? A walking flowerpot! Ah, ha, ha!"

Somehow or other the girl managed to survive. But her life was so miserable that as the years went by she began to wish she'd never been born. One day when she was nearly grown up, she came to a pier beside a river. She walked to the edge of the pier, sighed, and bowed her head.

"Mother," she prayed, "I'm sorry, but I can't go on like this. I want to be with you. Please show me the way to heaven!"

And with that she threw herself into the icy stream. But what do you think happened? The flowerpot floated to the surface and held the girl's head above water as she was swept helplessly along by the current.

She floated downstream all night before she was washed ashore to lie in the mud, exhausted. And that's where she was some hours later when a handsome young prince came riding by with his servants.

The prince spotted the girl and ordered his men to rescue her. Then, once he saw that she was safe and warm, he approached and spoke to her gently. He asked her where she was from and what she was called and, of course, why she was wearing a flowerpot. But the girl only stared at the ground and made no reply.

"Well, if you haven't anywhere to go, and I suspect you haven't," said the prince, "you can stay at our castle and work for us."

So from that day Flowerpot became a servant of the prince's family. The prince's father, a great samurai, was pleased to see how hard she worked, and even the other servants grew quite fond

of her. But the girl kept to herself and told no one her sad story.

One evening Flowerpot was cleaning a storeroom when she came across an old thirteen-stringed koto. Thinking back to the happy days when she used to play the koto

for her mother, she knelt down on the floor
and began to pluck the strings quietly.

It so happened that the young prince was
walking down the hallway just then, and he
stopped to listen. He had never heard the koto
played so beautifully before, and when he
walked into the room to see who the musician was, he couldn't believe his eyes.

"Flowerpot! Was that really you? Why, you
play the koto like a princess!" he exclaimed,
sitting down beside her. "You know, Flowerpot, I've always had a feeling about
you . . . You're not just an ordinary servant
girl, are you? Please tell me who you are and
where you're from."

Shyly, hesitatingly, the girl began her tale.

Her story astonished the prince, her gentle way of speaking touched his heart, and, much to his own surprise, he found himself falling in love.

That night the prince went to see his parents. "Mother, Father," he announced, "I've decided to marry."

"Why, that's wonderful, son. I'm sure we can arrange a splendid match for you."

"That won't be necessary. I'm going to marry the girl I found by the river."

"What!"

A servant who happened to overhear this rushed to Flowerpot to tell her the news.

"The prince?" she gasped. "The prince wants to marry *me*?" Surely, she thought, it must be a mistake. Or a cruel joke. Who would want a bride with a flowerpot stuck to her head?

Later, as she strolled through the garden deep in thought, Flowerpot heard voices coming from the house.

"Over my dead body!" the prince's father was shouting. "I'll never allow you to marry such a girl!"

"Please think it over, son," came his mother's voice. "There are so many nice young ladies you can choose from."

But the prince insisted he would marry no one but Flowerpot.

"Then you won't marry anyone at all!" roared his father, growing angrier by the moment.

When Flowerpot realized how upset the prince's parents were, she felt it was all her fault and decided to leave the castle forever. "He feels sorry for me, that's all," she thought. "Soon he'll forget I ever existed."

But as Flowerpot stole through the garden toward the front gate, the prince stepped outside and spotted her.

"Where are you going?" he cried, hurrying down the steps from the porch. "You mustn't leave! You're all I want in this world!" The prince ran to Flowerpot and caught her by the hand. But his father came running down the steps after him.

"I told you I'd have no more of this nonsense!" he yelled at his son. "If you won't forget the wench, then, by heaven, I'll have her head!" And with that he drew his long, sharp sword and stepped toward the girl.

"No, Father!"

"Get out of the way, boy!" The father pushed his son aside and raised the sword high over his head.

That's when it happened.

The flowerpot began to glow with a blinding, brilliant light. And a moment later, as if by magic, it shattered and fell to the ground in a million pieces.

The prince and his father stared in amazement. The flowerpot no one had ever been able to budge was suddenly gone and now,

for the first time, they saw the girl's face.

"F–Flowerpot," stammered the prince. "You . . . you really are a princess!"

His father, too, was stunned by Flowerpot's dazzling beauty. "Young lady," he said, "I owe you an apology. I can think of no one who would make a better bride for my son. Please accept his offer of marriage."

So Flowerpot married her prince and, of course, she lived happily ever after. And come to think of it, if it hadn't been for Kannon's strange advice, none of this would ever have happened.

The Snow Woman

Long ago in a small village in the cold, cold north country, a woodcutter named Mosaku lived with his son, Minokichi.

One freezing winter's morning, when the snow was too deep for cutting wood, Mosaku and Minokichi went hunting. They spent the entire day trudging through the mountains without spotting even so much as a rabbit. It was already late afternoon when, quite suddenly, great dark clouds rolled over the sky and snow began to fall, covering up the path and erasing the hunters' footprints behind them.

Although they could hardly see where they were going, they were lucky enough to stumble upon a woodcutters' hut. They decided to stay there until the storm blew over.

"We may have to spend the night here," said Mosaku as he stacked some wood in the fireplace.

"I'm afraid so, Father."

The two men sat talking beside the flickering fire while the wind howled around the door. It had been a long time since they'd had a good heart-to-heart talk, and the hours went quickly by. It was already quite late when Mosaku lay down on the floor facing his son.

"You know, son," he said, "when a man gets to be my age, he begins to want grandchildren. Isn't it time you thought about getting married?"

Minokichi blushed and stared dreamily at the fire. Little did he know that those were the last words his poor father would ever speak . . .

They were both very tired from their long day, and soon they were fast asleep. Outside, the snowstorm continued to rage. It was after midnight when an especially strong gust of wind suddenly blew the door ajar. Snow came swirling into the hut, putting out the fire.

Minokichi woke up shivering. "Brrr! It's f-freezing," he muttered, sitting up. That's

 when he saw her. She was standing in the shadows just inside the open door.

"Who is it? Who's there?"

Out of the shadows stepped a beautiful woman dressed in flowing white silk. Her hair was long and black, and her skin was as pale and smooth as polished ivory. But as he looked into her cold, dark eyes, Minokichi felt a shiver run down his spine.

The woman ignored him, however, and walked slowly toward his father, who was still asleep. Minokichi watched helplessly as the woman bent down and exhaled a frosty white cloud that hung over Mosaku like a hungry ghost.

"Father!" he cried, trembling with fear. "Father!" But there was no response. The woman turned and moved toward Minokichi.

"Help! Help!" Minokichi stood up to run, but the woman stepped in front of him, blocking his path. She stared deep into his eyes and, to his horror and bewilderment, her cruel gaze softened and a tender smile formed on her lips.

"You are young and full of life," she whispered. "Youth is a wonderful thing. I shall let you live. But remember: if you ever tell anyone about tonight, you too shall die."

Another gust of wind and snow swirled around the room, and the woman was gone. Minokichi's knees buckled, and he fell to the floor unconscious.

Had it been some terrible dream? Perhaps. But Minokichi awoke in the morning to find the door open, the fire out, and his father lying next to him, frozen to death.

Most of the people in the village came to Mosaku's funeral to pay their respects and to comfort Minokichi. "It was the worst blizzard I've ever seen," Minokichi told them, shaking his head sadly and wiping the tears from his eyes. But he told no one about the mysterious woman in white.

A year passed, and another winter came and went. One dark and rainy spring day, Minokichi looked out his window and noticed a young lady sheltering beneath the eaves of his house. Seeing she had no umbrella, he invited her to wait inside until the rain stopped.

The young lady's name, Minokichi learned, was Yuki. She told him she was on her way

to the capital. When he found out she was traveling alone, Minokichi offered to help her in any way he could. They drank tea and talked on and on. And almost before either of them realized it, they had fallen deeply in love.

Yuki never did get to the capital. She stayed with Minokichi, and they were married soon after. It seemed a match made in heaven. As time went by they were blessed with five healthy, handsome children. Yuki was a cheerful, devoted wife and mother, and Minokichi was happier than he had ever been in his life. The only thing that ever really worried him was his wife's delicate health. On hot summer days Yuki would grow weak and listless. But Minokichi always cared for her lovingly, and the cool breezes of evening never failed to revive her.

One night, as Yuki was doing her sewing, Mino-kichi looked at her and thought for the thousandth time how lovely she was. "Yuki," he said, "you haven't changed at all. You seem as young and beautiful as the day we met." Gazing at her profile, he suddenly remembered something that had happened long ago. Something he'd never told anyone about. "You know, I just realized," he said, "you remind me a lot of someone I once saw. Or thought I saw."

"Oh? Who was she?" asked Yuki, looking up from her sewing.

"Well, I told you about the blizzard my father and I were caught in when I was twenty. That's when I saw her. I'm still not sure it wasn't just a dream, but . . ." Minokichi hesitated. "Have you ever heard those stories about the Snow Woman?"

"You had to say it, didn't you?" Yuki's voice was a harsh whisper, and there was a funny look in her eyes. "And you promised. You promised you wouldn't tell anyone."

"What do you mean? Yuki, what's the matter? Where are you going?"

Yuki had stood up and was walking toward the

door. And as she moved, her kimono began turning white. White as snow . . .

"Yuki," Minokichi gasped. "Yuki, you . . . you're . . ."

Yes. Yuki was the legendary Snow Woman. And now that Minokichi had broken his promise, she had no choice: she must either leave or destroy him. Fortunately, not even the Snow Woman could bring herself to kill the only man she had ever loved.

"Yuki! Don't go!" cried Minokichi, running after her.

"Why, Minokichi? Why did you say it? I wanted to stay with you. I wanted to be your wife forever . . ." Yuki's cold, dark eyes filled with tears. "I'll never forget you, Minokichi. I'll never forget the happiness I've known with you. Take good care of yourself, and the children . . . Goodbye, my love."

The door flew open and a cold wind rushed through the

room. Then there was silence, and Yuki had vanished. Minokichi ran out the door to the empty street.

"Yuki! Yuki-i-i!"

Minokichi was never to see his wife again. But people in the north country say that on cold, snowy nights, the one they call *Yuki Onna*—the Snow Woman—still wanders the mountainsides, crying out in a chilling whine. She's searching, they say, for a man who will keep her secret safe and her cold heart warm.

Tengu's Vanishing Cloak

Once upon a time there was a very clever and very mischievous little boy named Hikohachi, who was always dreaming up new ways of getting into trouble.

Now Hikohachi had often heard tell of a goblin known as Tengu who lived in the nearby mountain forest. This Tengu, it was said, had a wonderful cloak that could make anyone wearing it invisible. What fun it would be, Hikohachi often thought, if he could get his hands on that vanishing cloak!

Well, one day he had an idea. He hollowed out a piece of bamboo and carried it up the

47

mountain where Tengu was said to live. When he reached the top of the mountain, he began to peer through the bamboo tube.

"Wow!" he cried in a loud voice. "You can see forever. This is great!"

It wasn't long before he heard a rustling in the trees. Hikohachi was sure it was Tengu come to watch him. He smiled to himself and continued to shout.

"I can see all the way to Osaka!"

Finally a raspy voice came from the top of a pine tree. "Say, boy. Let me see that thing."

Hikohachi acted surprised. "Hey! Who said that?"

"It's me. Tengu. Let me see that thing you've got there, will you?"

"No way!" said Hikohachi, shaking his head. "This is my greatest treasure. It's the most powerful spyglass in the whole world."

Tengu slid down the tree. "Come on, boy. Please? Just one tiny little peek."

"Uh-unh. This

spyglass is the only one of its kind. You think I'll let just anyone look through it?"

"Tell you what," said Tengu. "I'll let you play with this cloak of mine."

"Ha! What do I want with a dirty old cloak like that?"

"Dirty? Listen here, boy. This cloak can make you invisible. How's that for a treasure? Come on. Let me see that spyglass thing."

"Well . . ." Hikohachi pretended to be thinking it over. Finally he sighed and said, "All right. But just for a minute."

"Now you're talking. Hand it over."

"Give me the cloak first."

They made the swap, and Tengu held the hollow piece of bamboo up to his eye. Hikohachi, meanwhile, slipped the cloak over his head and vanished.

"Say, boy," said Tengu. "I don't see anything . . . Boy?" He looked all

about, but Hikohachi was nowhere to be found. "Boy! Where'd you go?"

Hikohachi was already scurrying down the mountain, testing the vanishing cloak by playing tricks on all the animals that crossed his path. And it worked! Not even the animals could see him.

"I can't wait to try it out on people!" he thought.

That evening, in the town near the village where Hikohachi lived, strange things began to happen. One man, for example, was walking down the main street with a heavy load on his back when someone tripped him.

"Who did that?" he growled, picking himself up off the ground. "Who's the wise guy?"

A few moments later, a fat lady shrieked and held her nose, claiming that someone had just pinched her there. A pretty girl on the corner had her ears tweaked and let out a squeal. And a bald man dozing in front of his store was surprised by a big slap on the forehead.

Fights started breaking out.

"Ow! You kicked me!"

"Me? You're the one who poked me in the eye!"

At the fish market an octopus began dancing in midair, driving away all the frightened customers. Dumplings disappeared from the counter at a tea shop, and a hand drum floated down the street by itself.

The cause of all this confusion, of course, was Hikohachi and his vanishing cloak. He was having the time of his life. Soon it began to grow late, however, and he had to head back to his village. When he got home, he called for his grandmother.

"Grandma, I'm home! Come here, I want to show you something."

Hikohachi's grandmother came outside wiping her hands and shaking her head. "Hikohachi," she said, "I'm too busy to—Hm? Where is that boy? Tsk. Forever playing tricks . . ."

The old woman walked back into the house muttering to herself. And there, just inside the doorway, stood Hikohachi.

"Something wrong with your eyes, Grandma?" he teased. "I've been standing right here the whole time!"

That night Hikohachi put the vanishing cloak in the garden storehouse and went to bed. But he was so excited just thinking about all the tricks he'd play the next day that he didn't get to sleep until very late.

When he awoke in

the morning the sun was already high. Rubbing his eyes, he walked out into the garden, where he found his grandmother standing next to a pile of burning rubbish.

"Well, sleepyhead," she said, "you finally got up."

Hikohachi gasped and his mouth fell open. In his grandmother's hands was Tengu's cloak, and she was just about to throw it into the fire!

"No!" he shouted. "Don't burn that!"

"This dirty old rag? Don't be silly. I won't have it in my house," she said. "Where did you get such a filthy thing?" And into the fire it went.

Hikohachi was crushed. But as he stood watching his precious cloak go up in flames, a brilliant idea came to him. He waited until the cloak had burned and his grandmother had gone back into the house. Then he took off his clothes and spread the ashes from the fire all over

his body. And sure enough, he began to disappear. Soon he was completely invisible.

"Ha!" he cried. "I'm a genius! This is even better than wearing that heavy old cloak."

Hikohachi hurried off to town, chuckling to himself. He was running down the main street again, pinching noses and tweaking ears, when he came screeching to a halt. Right in front of his eyes was a big pile of manju—sweet bean-jam buns.

"Oh, boy!" he thought. "A manju shop!"

There was nothing Hikohachi loved more than manju. He began gobbling them down one after the other, licking the sweet jam from his lips as he ate. Unfortunately, he also licked off all the ash around his mouth. And when the man who owned the shop finally noticed his manju were disappearing, he stepped outside to find two pink lips floating in the air.

"Aaaggghhh!" he shout-ed. "A g–g–ghost! And it's stealing my manju. Stop thief!"

Hikohachi dashed off, laughing, and the manju man ran

54

after him, along with several other people who happened to be standing nearby. "Stop!" they yelled. "Stop those spooky lips!"

Hikohachi was running as fast as he could, and soon he broke out in a sweat. As the sweat ran down his body, it washed off the ashes in streaks. Little by little, parts of him became visible, and he began to look more like a ghost than ever.

Half the people in town were running after Hikohachi now. They were right behind him when he reached the river. There was nothing for him to do but jump in.

Splash!

When Hikohachi came up for air, of course, the ash was all gone and everyone could see who he was. The fun and games were over.

He spent the next day, and every day for weeks after that, working at different stores in town to pay for the damage he'd done. He came to wish he'd never heard of Tengu and his vanishing cloak.

Oh, and what about Tengu? Well, they say he's still at the top of his pine tree, trying to see Osaka through that bamboo tube.

Grandfather Cherry Blossom

Once upon a time a kind old man lived with his gentle wife in a village at the foot of a mountain. The old man was plowing his field one day when he heard someone shouting. It was the greedy old grouch who lived next door.

"Bah! Get out of my garden!"

Yip! Yip! Yip! A little white puppy came running toward the old man and jumped in-to his arms just as the grouchy neighbor appeared.

"That mutt was tearing up my garden. Hand him over!" demanded the neighbor.

The frightened puppy was shaking and whimpering. "I'm sure he didn't mean any harm. Won't you overlook it just this once?"

The kind old man smiled and bowed. "I'll make sure he doesn't bother you any more."

"Suit yourself," grumbled the grouch, walking away angrily. "But if I ever see that stupid dog in my garden again, I'll kill him."

The kind old man and his wife decided to keep the stray puppy. They named him Shiro, which means "white," because his fur was the color of fresh-fallen snow.

Now Shiro had a very big appetite, and the kind old couple always gave him as much food as he could eat. The more he ate the larger he grew, and soon he was so big he could carry the old man on his back.

One morning, as the old man was hoeing his field, Shiro came and tugged at his sleeve, as if he wanted to show him something.

"What is it, Shiro? I'm kind of busy, boy."

But Shiro wouldn't leave him alone. Finally the old man climbed on the huge dog's back and off they went, up the mountain behind the house. When they neared the top, Shiro stopped next to a tree and begin barking.

"Arf, arf! Dig here! Arf, arf!"

The old man scratched his head, shrugged, and started to dig with his hoe. Before long he struck something hard.

"Hm? What's this?" He kneeled down and reached into the hole. "Why, it's . . . it's gold! Gold coins, and lots of them!"

That night the old man and his wife were sitting at home talking excitedly about how Shiro had found the treasure, when the greedy old grouch happened by with his even greedier old wife. They peeked through a hole in the door and spotted the pile of gold. When the grouch overheard the story, he was green with envy. He found Shiro, threw a rope around his neck, and dragged the dog home with him.

The next day, the old grouch and his wife jumped on Shiro's back and drove him up the mountain, kicking and whipping him mercilessly. They had almost neared the peak when Shiro's strength gave out and he fell over, panting.

"This must be the spot!" cried the greedy old man. He started digging, and before very long—*clank!*—his hoe struck something hard. "Hooray! We did it! We're rich!"

Convinced that he had found gold, the old grouch reached into the hole. What came out, however, weren't gold bars at all but slimy snakes—*Hisssss, hisssss*—and weird, smelly goblins—*Wooooo!*

The old grouch and his wife screamed and fell back, covering their eyes. When they finally opened them, the snakes and goblins were gone and their fear gave way to rage.

"Look what you've done, you stupid dog!" yelled the grouch. "I'll teach you not to make a fool of me again!" He picked up his hoe and gave Shiro such a blow over the head that it killed the poor dog instantly.

The kind old man and woman, of course, were heartbroken when they learned what had happened. They carried Shiro down from the mountain and buried him near their home. Next to the grave they planted a little tree, and after saying a prayer for the dog they had loved so much, they went home with tears in their eyes.

That might have been the end of the story. But soon a wondrous thing began to happen. The tree the old couple had planted started to grow at an unbelievable speed. In no time at all it was so large you couldn't reach around it.

One morning the old man and his wife were putting fresh flowers on Shiro's grave when they looked up at the great tree and marveled at how it had grown. And at that moment something even more wondrous happened.

They heard a voice coming from inside the trunk. "Make me into a mortar," it seemed to be saying. "Make me into a mortar . . ."

The old man scratched his head, shrugged, and went to the house to get his axe. He cut down the tree and shaped part of the trunk into a large mortar for pounding mochi—soft rice cakes.

"Come to think of it, Shiro always loved mochi, didn't he?" said the gentle old woman when they got the mortar home. "Let's make some to put on his grave."

"That's a good idea,"

Oomph! Ah! Oomph! Ah! The old man pounded the rice in the mortar with a heavy wooden mallet, and after each swing his wife kneaded the gradually thickening dough. It was getting smooth and sticky when suddenly the old woman stopped and pointed inside the mortar. Something was glittering in there.

"Look, dear," she said. "What's that?"

"I don't know. I've never seen mochi like this."

They took the dough out of the mortar and rolled it into little round cakes. And as they watched, the mochi hardened and began to shine even more brightly.

"Why, this isn't mochi," the old man cried. "It's gold!"

So it was. And who should show his face again just at that moment but the greedy old grouch from next door. He and his wife had been peeping in the whole time. "Say," he said, "how about lending me that mortar?"

"But . . . but this is all that's left of dear old Shiro . . ."

"You'll get it back. Don't be so stingy." The grouch and his wife walked right in and carried the mortar away. And as soon as they got home, they started to pound their own mochi.

The greedy old woman kept peering inside the mortar. "It hasn't changed color at all," she said. "I know—we've got to shape it into little cakes."

So that's just what they did, placing the small round pieces in a row on the table. And sure enough, right before their eyes, the mochi began to change—but not into gold. It became a mass of gooey black charcoal. The old grouch and his wife stared at the mess in disgust and were just about to begin yelling at each other when—*poof!*—the charcoal ex-

ploded, filling the kitchen with flames and black soot. Sputtering and shouting, the grouch grabbed his axe, chopped the mortar into tiny bits, and threw the pieces into the fire.

The kindhearted old man broke down and cried when he heard what had happened. He went to the grouch's house, gathered up the ashes of the mortar, and placed them in a basket. "Shiro . . ." he sobbed as he carried the basket home.

His gentle wife tried to comfort him. "Let's scatter these ashes on the field," she said, "and grow some of those giant radishes that Shiro used to love so much." The old man agreed

and they walked slowly out to the field with the basket.

Now it was a very windy day, and as the old man was scattering the ashes, some of them blew onto a withered old cherry tree. And that's when the most wondrous thing of all happened.

No sooner had the ashes fallen on the tree than the dry branches sprang back to life and became covered with beautiful blossoms.

"Goodness gracious! Come quick, dear. Watch this!"

As his wife looked on, the old man ran about sprinkling ashes on cherry trees. And every tree touched by the ashes began to bloom. Soon the little field was alive with colorful flowers.

In the days that followed, all the people in the village came to marvel at this wonderful sight. "Such lovely cherry blossoms," they would say. "And it's not even spring!"

The word spread like wildfire from village to village, until it reached the ears of a great daimyo. Once he'd heard of this miracle, the daimyo decided he must see it with his own eyes. Taking ten or twelve of his best soldiers, he made the long journey over the mountains to the little village where the old man lived. When he got to the house, the old man came out, bowing, to greet him.

"I've heard a lot about you, old man," said the daimyo. "Let me see what you can do."

The old man climbed up a withered cherry tree. "If it please your lordship," he announced, "I'll make this dead cherry tree come back to life and bloom."

And that's exactly what he did, much to

the daimyo's amazement. The ashes he sprinkled on the branches turned, in the twinkling of an eye, into lovely pink and white flowers.

"Extraordinary! I've never seen anything like it!" the daimyo exclaimed. "Old man, you're the best blossom-maker in the land. Henceforth, sir, you shall be known as Grandfather Cherry Blossom. Allow me to reward you with this." The daimyo held out a sack full of silver and gold.

"Just a moment, your lordship!" came a familiar voice. The greedy old grouch from next door ran up to the daimyo and bowed. "I'm the real Grandfather Cherry Blossom. Watch this . . ." He snatched the basket from the kindhearted old man, climbed a tree, and threw the ashes into the air.

But instead of turning into blossoms, the ashes merely fell toward the ground, and a gust of wind blew them right into the daimyo's face. The daimyo sneezed and coughed, rubbed his eyes, and brushed the ashes off his clothes. He was enraged. "Arrest that old impostor!" he shouted to his soldiers.

So the grouch was tied up and carted off to jail. And it served him right, don't you think?

Tanabata

Across the sky of a clear summer night, the Milky Way flows like a mighty river. On either side of its vast, raging current are the bright stars Altair and Vega. According to an old legend, these two heavenly bodies were once an earthly man and his wife. Now, it is said, they are allowed to meet only once a year—on the seventh day of the seventh month. This is the story of those star-crossed lovers.

Once upon a time a young man named Mikeran was walking home after working in the fields. As

he passed by the
shore of a lake, he
spotted something
hanging from a
tree.

"What's that?"
he wondered. "It
looks like a robe. . . ."

But it was not like any robe he had seen
before. It shone like a star in the evening light.
Mikeran was delighted with his find. "It must
be worth a fortune," he thought. He took the
robe down, folded it up, and placed it in his
basket. He was about to walk away when
someone called out to him.

"Excuse me, sir.'"

"What? Who said that?"

"I did." Out of the tall grass by the lake stepped the most beautiful young woman Mikeran
had ever seen. "Please," she said. "Please give
me back my celestial robe."

"C-celestial robe?"

"Yes. Oh, please, sir. Without it I can't
return to my home in heaven. You see," she
went on, her eyes brimming with tears, "I
don't belong on earth. I only came here to

bathe a while in this lovely lake. Please, I beg you, give me back my robe!"

Mikeran's heart was beating wildly. "I-I don't know what you're talking about," he lied. "I haven't seen any robe."

The truth is that Mikeran had fallen in love the moment he'd laid eyes on the maiden. He feared that if he gave her the robe, she'd fly off into the sky and disappear forever.

"Shall I help you look for it?" he said.

"Oh, would you, sir?"

Mikeran pretended to search for the robe, but, of course, it was in his basket all the time. "It's no use," he said at last. "Someone must have stolen it."

Tanabata—for that was the maiden's name—sat on the ground and began to sob.

"Don't cry," said Mikeran, taking her hand. "If you've nowhere to go, you can come stay with me."

So from that day on, Tanabata lived in Mikeran's house. And as time went by she came to love the gentle, handsome youth as much as he loved her. They were married and spent many wonderful years together. Happy as she was with her earthly life,

however, Tanabata could never forget her home in heaven. Often at night when Mikeran was asleep she would open the window and gaze up, sighing, at the starry sky.

Then, one day when Mikeran was out working in the fields, Tanabata noticed her pet dove pecking at something between the roofbeams. As she watched, the dove thrust its beak into a crack in the ceiling and pulled out a piece of beautiful, glittering cloth.

"My robe!" Tanabata cried. "So Mikeran knew where it was all along. He was hiding it from me!"

That evening Mikeran returned from the fields to find his wife waiting outside in her celestial garment.

"Tanabata! You—you found the robe!"

Tanabata nodded sadly, lifted her hands toward heaven, and began to rise in the air.

As she rose, she looked down at her husband and said, "Mikeran . . . if you really love me, weave a thousand pairs of straw sandals and bury them beneath a bamboo shoot. If you do that, we'll be able to meet again. I'll be waiting for you, my love . . ."

Mikeran watched helplessly as Tanabata ascended higher and higher. At last all he could see was her robe shining like a star in the evening sky.

Mikeran knew he would never be happy until he was reunited with his beautiful wife. So that very night he gathered all the straw he could find and began to weave the sandals. Night and day, day and night, he weaved and counted, counted and weaved.

At last he counted a thousand pairs. He hurried outside, found a bamboo shoot, and

dug a large hole for the sandals beneath it. No sooner had he covered the sandals with earth than the bamboo began to grow at an incredible speed. In a matter of seconds, the tip had disappeared into the clouds.

"Now all I have to do is climb to the top!" thought Mikeran. From one branch to the next he climbed and climbed and climbed. And when finally he got to the top, he could see heaven's floor just above him. But he couldn't quite reach it. It seems that in his haste to meet Tanabata, he had made a mistake when he counted the sandals. He'd actually only woven nine hundred and ninety-nine pairs.

"Tanabata!" he shouted. "Tanabata, are you there?"

Tanabata was working her loom when she heard someone calling her name. "Oh!" she gasped. "Can it be?" She peered over the edge of her cloud and there, sure enough, was her husband, waving to her from the top of the great bamboo.

"Mikeran! Hold on!" Tanabata took the long piece of cloth from her loom and lowered it to Mikeran. He grabbed hold of it, pulled

himself up to her cloud, and ran to her.

"Tanabata! I missed you so much!"

"Oh, Mikeran!"

They were holding each other tenderly when a bearded and fearful-looking old man appeared. It was Tanabata's father.

"What is the meaning of this?" he roared.

"This is my husband, Father," said Tanabata meekly. "His name is Mikeran."

"I'm honored to meet you, sir," said Mikeran, bowing.

But Tanabata's father was not at all happy to learn that his daughter had married a lowly earthling. "Tell me, young man," he said with a scowl, "how did you make your living on earth?"

"I worked in the fields, sir."

"Good. I've got just the job for you, then. Take all the seeds in those baskets and plant them in the star-field. You have three days to finish."

"Y–yes, sir," gulped Mikeran.

There must have been a million seeds in the huge baskets. Mikeran set to work immediately, and for three days he never even stopped to rest. Finally, late on the third day, he planted the last seed and lay down exhausted. But no sooner had he done so than Tanabata's father appeared again.

"Not *this* star-field, you fool!" he shouted. "I meant the star-field over *there*. Now pick up all those seeds and replant them!"

Poor Mikeran. It would take years to find all the seeds. Luckily, however, Tanabata had an idea. She called for her pet dove. "I want you to bring all your friends," she told the bird. "Ask them to dig out those seeds and replant them."

Before long the skies were filled with thousands of doves diving and swooping and soaring from one star-field to the other. And the job was finished in no time at all.

Tanabata's father was not amused, however. He spent the night thinking up another difficult task for Mikeran, and in the morning he called the earthling before him. "I need you to stand guard over the melon patch in the Valley of Heaven," he said. "You must remain there for three days and three nights. And you're not to eat or drink anything while you're there."

When Tanabata heard of this new command, she was very worried. "Do be careful, Mikeran," she said. "And whatever you do, don't eat any of the sacred melons. If you do, something terrible will happen. Please promise me you won't."

Mikeran swore he wouldn't touch the sacred fruit. But after two days of guarding the patch in the scorching sun, his throat was so parched he thought he would die of thirst. At last he couldn't stand it any longer. He cut open one of the ripe, juicy melons.

Ssshhhwwwoooooosssshhh!

A great torrent of water came gushing

78

out of the melon. And in the twinkling of an
eye the torrent became a raging river. Mikeran
was swept off his feet, and the powerful current carried him to the far side of the Valley
of Heaven.

"Mikera-a-an!"

"Tanabata-a-a!"

To this day, Tanabata and Mikeran sit on
opposite banks of the river we call the Milky
Way. You can see them each night gazing
helplessly across at each
other, waiting for the
one day in the year her
father allows them to
meet.

Bunbuku Teakettle

Long, long ago, at Morinji Temple in Gunma Prefecture, there lived a certain priest who loved nothing more than collecting curios. One day this priest returned to the temple with an old teakettle he'd bought in town. He went straight to his room and inspected his purchase carefully. He even sniffed at it.

Sniff, sniff. "Hm . . . Smells a little funny," he said, wrinkling his nose. "Yoo-hoo! Where is everybody?"

Two of the young boys who lived and studied at the temple came running. "Yes, Master?"

"I want you to clean this

80

teakettle for me. Use plenty of sand, and polish it till it's nice and shiny."

The boys carried the kettle outside, grumbling. "Why doesn't he clean it himself?" they complained. They were slapping handfuls of wet sand on the teakettle and scrubbing away recklessly when something incredible happened: the kettle jumped out of their hands and screamed.

"Ouch! That hurts!"

"Aaaiiieee!" The boys leaped up and ran to the priest, stumbling and falling over each other.

"M–Master! Help!"

"The teakettle . . . It t-talked!"

The priest, of course, didn't believe them. "You'll do anything to get out of a little work, won't you?" he scolded. "You ought to be ashamed of yourselves, coming to me with a story like that. Enough of this nonsense! Fill the kettle with water and bring it here."

Reluctantly, the boys did as they were told.

They rinsed the kettle out carefully, filled it with water, and carried it to the priest's room. The priest set it over the fire, and the boys backed away, trembling with fear.

Sitting on the fire, however, it looked to the priest like any old teakettle. "Hmph. Always coming up with ridiculous stories, aren't you?" he said, scowling. "Talking teakettles, indeed! That'll be the day!"

Well, no sooner had he said this than there was a loud cry—"Ow! It's hot!"—and the teakettle began shaking and spurting out water, making a sound like this: *Bun-buku, sssss! Bun-buku, sssss!*

The boys ran screaming out of the room, and it was all the horrified priest could do to keep from running with them. However much he loved curios, he wanted no part of a talking teakettle. It was the spookiest thing he'd ever seen, and he decided to get rid of it as soon as possible.

As luck would have it, a poor tinker was passing by just at that moment.

"I know," thought the priest. "I'll give it to him." He stepped outside

and waved. "Hallo-o! Mr. Tinker!"

When the tinker was told he could have the teakettle, he was overjoyed. "You're going to give me this kettle for free?" he said. "Well, how do you like that? My luck must be changing at last." He tucked the teakettle under his arm and headed for home, humming contentedly.

And that wasn't the end of the tinker's apparent good fortune. Later that evening a friend of his stopped by his house with a most welcome gift: a large, freshly caught fish.

"I haven't eaten a whole fish in years," the tinker thought as he grilled it over the fire. "First the teakettle and now this. What a day!" But when he sat down at the table after washing his hands . . .

"Oh, no! My fish is gone!" The meal he had so looked forward to eating had vanished. He searched everywhere, but the fish was nowhere to be found. "Isn't that just my luck? I'm about to celebrate getting this nice little teakettle and my dinner disappears. Oh, well. It won't be the first time I've gone to sleep on an empty stomach."

Sighing, the tinker got ready for bed. No sooner did he lay down and close his eyes, however, than a voice in the darkness said, "Forgive me, Mr. Tinker. I'm the one who ate your fish." The startled man sat up and opened his eyes. And guess what he saw. The teakettle was sprouting the head, legs, and tail of a tanuki!

"It's alive!" shouted the tinker. He was getting ready to run outside when the teakettle spoke to him again.

"I didn't mean to frighten you. I'm really

just a plain old tanuki—and not a very clever one, either."

"What? Oh, now I get it. So you're only a tanuki who turned himself into a teakettle. Phew! You did give me quite a scare, you little rascal."

"I'm really sorry about eating that fish."

"Oh, that's all right. Forget it. You must have been hungry."

No one had ever spoken so kindly to the tanuki before. His little eyes filled with tears. "You're such a nice man," he sobbed. "Can I stay here with you?"

"Don't be silly. Look how poor I am. I can't afford to keep you. You'd better go back to the mountains where you belong."

But the tanuki, still sobbing, shook his head and said, "You don't understand. When I was in the mountains, my friends and I had a turning-into-things contest. But I was the only one who couldn't turn back into a proper tanuki. I can't go home like this—I'm too ashamed!"

"All right, look," said the tinker. "I'll put you up for tonight. But in the morning you'll have to go."

The next day, however, the tanuki plead-ed with him again.

"Please let me stay. If it's money you're wor-ried about, I can earn my keep."

"You? How?"

"I can perform tricks. All you have to do, Mr. Tinker, is make a little show tent, and people will pay to watch me."

It seemed like a crazy idea, but the tanuki was very persuasive. Soon the tinker was set-ting up a tent in the front yard. And the very next day they gave their first public performance.

"Come one, come all. See the tanuki tightrope-walker with the wondrous and amusing name—Bunbuku Teakettle!" The teakettle-tanuki danced on the high wire to the beat of the tinker's drum, and the crowd roared with delight.

Before long, Bunbuku Teakettle's antics on the tightrope had become the talk of the countryside. People came from far and wide to watch his show, and the money poured in. Soon the tinker was living a life of luxury. Of course, he never forgot that he owed it all to his little friend.

One night the tinker was in his room reading a book. Bunbuku came in, sat down beside him, and asked, "What are you doing?"

"I'm trying to find a way to help you turn back into a real tanuki. You've done so much for me, and now I want to do something for you."

The teakettle-tanuki shook his head. "No!" he cried. "I like it the way I am. I'm enjoying myself every day!"

Two years passed. They were the two happiest years of Bunbuku's life. During this time, the tinker continued to try to find some way to free his little friend from the teakettle, but nothing worked. Bunbuku, meanwhile, never tired of repeating that he liked being just the way he was.

Having a kettle for a body would be hard on anyone, though. One very cold winter's day, Bunbuku collapsed with a dangerously high fever.

The tinker tried his best to nurse him back to health and to cheer him up. "Bunbuku," he would say, "in the spring, when you're better, we'll go see the cherry blossoms. Won't that be fun? We'll take some rice cakes with us and we'll sing songs and dance, and . . ."

The teakettle-tanuki's eyes would fill with tears of joy as he listened to the tinker's kind words. But he knew it was not to be. One night

he called his friend to his bedside and whispered a short, painful goodbye.

"Bunbuku!" cried the tinker. "Please don't die!" But it was too late. The teakettle-tanuki had breathed his last.

In the morning, the tinker sadly carried his lifeless teakettle back to the curio-loving priest. Impressed by Bunbuku's amazing story, the priest promised to keep the kettle as one of Morinji Temple's most valued treasures. And that's where it remains to this day.

Earless Ho-ichi

Long ago the town of Shimonoseki was known as Akama. On the outskirts of Akama stood Amida Temple. And in this temple lived a musical monk named Ho-ichi.

Ho-ichi had been blind since birth. As a child, he learned to play a kind of lute called the biwa. He studied and practiced very hard, and now, though still young, he was a great master of the instrument. People came from all over the country to hear Ho-ichi perform the epic tale of the famous Heike clan. They especially loved the way he sang the last part of the tale, about the great Battle of Dannoura.

90

The Battle of Dannoura took place at sea, in the Straits of Shimonoseki. It marked the end of the long, bloody feud between the Heike and Genji clans. The battle ended with the defeat of the Heike, most of whom were killed. And among the victims was the eight-year-old Emperor Antoku. It's a tragic tale indeed, and when Ho-ichi played and sang it, no one could listen without shedding a tear.

One hot, humid summer night, the priest and the other monks of Amida Temple all went off to chant sutras at a funeral in town. Ho-ichi was alone in the temple playing the biwa when he heard someone call his name.

"Ho-ichi! Ho-ichi!"

"Who's there? Who is it?"

"I am the messenger of a great lord who lives nearby," answered the voice. "His lordship has learned of your skill with the biwa and wishes to hear you play and sing. Follow me and I'll lead you to the castle."

Ho-ichi was thrilled that such an illustrious person wanted to hear his music. He eagerly followed the messenger, whose armor clanked and rattled. No doubt the messenger himself was a dashing and noble samurai.

At length they passed through a large gate, across a spacious garden, and into an enormous banquet hall. A great crowd of people seemed to be gathered there. Ho-ichi could hear the rustle of silks and the clatter of armor on all sides.

"We've been waiting for you, Ho-ichi," came the gentle voice of a woman. "Please sing the tale of the Heike for us."

"As you wish, your ladyship."

Ho-ichi took a seat and began to sing and pluck at his biwa. Never before had he played with such emotion. When he came to the final battle scene, he sang of the waves crashing over the decks, of the twanging bow strings and the cries and shouts of the doomed warriors. And his biwa echoed each sound so

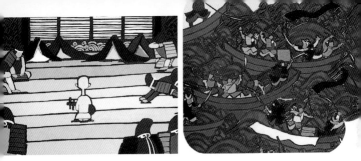

faithfully that the listeners felt as if they were reliving that fateful fight. They were all deeply moved. Gradually the hall filled with muffled sobs, and when Ho-Ichi had finished, no one spoke for some time.

"Ho-ichi," said the gentlewoman at last, "that was very beautiful. His lordship, also, has asked me to express his appreciation."

"The pleasure and honor are mine," said Ho-ichi, bowing.

"So pleased was his lordship, in fact," the lady went on, "that he wants you to return each night this week to play for us. You will be handsomely rewarded. But you must not mention this to anyone. Is that understood?"

After solemnly giving his word, Ho-ichi took leave of the company and was escorted back to the temple.

The next night the samurai messenger came

again to lead Ho-ichi to the castle. Again he played and sang the Heike tale, and again the lords and ladies wept.

This time Ho-ichi didn't get back to the temple till the dawn. The priest saw him returning and asked where he'd been all night, but Ho-ichi remembered his promise and refused to answer. This made the priest suspicious, and he ordered the monks to keep an eye on the blind man.

That night there was a tremendous thunderstorm. Two monks were sitting by an open door, watching the rain pour down, when they spotted Ho-ichi leaving the temple. They immediately set out to follow him as instructed. But blind Ho-ichi moved so quickly through the darkness that he left the two monks far behind.

"Where could he have gone?"

"I don't know. But we've got to find him."

After searching for over an hour in the pouring rain, however, they gave up and headed back to the temple. They were taking a shortcut through the cemetery when a great streak of lightning lit up the sky.

"L-look!" cried one of the monks. "It's Ho-ichi!"

The two men froze with fear at the sight before them. In front of the grave of the Emperor Antoku sat Ho-ichi with his biwa. And all around him danced dozens of phantom lights! These, the monks realized, were the spirits of the Heike who had perished in the nearby sea so long ago. Little did the blind musician know who he was playing for.

Seeing the danger Ho-ichi was in, the two monks ran to rescue him. With the ghostly lights buzzing around them like angry bees, they grabbed the blind man and dragged him out of the cemetery and back to the temple.

The next day, when the priest heard what had happened, he was beside himself with worry. He summoned Ho-ichi, called for a brush and ink, and proceeded to write Buddhist sutras all over the blind man's body.

When he'd written the last of the holy words, he laid down his brush and said, "Ho-ichi, tonight I must go to town again and I won't be here to help you. These sutras I've written on your body will make you invisible to spirits. But you are in great danger. You must do exactly as I tell you. If anyone should come and speak to you, do not answer them. Sit quietly in meditation and don't move a muscle. Your life depends upon it!"

"Yes, Master."

That night Ho-ichi was meditating alone in the temple when he heard the samurai messenger's voice.

"Ho-ichi . . . Ho-ichi . . ."

But the blind man sat perfectly still and made no reply. And all the ghostly messenger could see were two ears floating in the air. That's right. The priest had forgotten to brush the holy words over Ho-ichi's ears!

"I guess he's not here," sighed the ghost.

"Looks like he left his ears behind, though. I'd better take these back with me to prove I tried to find him."

The ghost took an ear in each hand and pulled. *Rip!* He peeled them right off Ho-ichi's head! Terrible as the pain was, however, Ho-ichi remembered the priest's warning and didn't move or make a sound.

When the priest returned to the temple in

the morning, he hurried to Ho-ichi's room to see if he was all right. And as soon as he saw the blood on the sides of the blind man's head, he realized what had happened. "Ah, Ho-ichi," he moaned. "You poor fellow. I forgot to write on your ears!"

But at least Ho-ichi was still alive, and the spirits never came back to bother him. Though he'd lost both ears, he continued to play the biwa and sing. He became more famous than ever, and before long there wasn't a soul in the country who hadn't heard of Earless Ho-ichi, the musical priest.

The Gratitude of the Crane

Once upon a time a kindhearted old man lived with his wife in a little house deep in the woods. The old couple were happy with their simple, quiet life, although it did get a bit lonely at times. They often thought how nice it would be if only they had a child of their own.

One day, as usual, the old man went out to gather firewood in the mountains near his home. He was on his way back that evening when he heard what sounded like a cry for help. He followed the sound to a frozen marsh by the side of the road. And there he found a beautiful white crane with its leg caught in a hunter's trap.

The old man got down on his knees and opened the trap to set the crane free. It flapped its wings, cried out for joy, and flew off into the snow-filled sky.

That night, sitting before the fire, the old man told his wife what had happened. "How happy that crane looked!" he chuckled. The old woman smiled, and they sat chatting idly and thinking pleasant thoughts until it was time to go to bed. They were about to do just that when someone knocked at the front door.

Knock, knock. Knock, knock.

Who could it be so late at night, so deep in the woods, and with all that snow outside?

Knock, knock.

The old man went to the door and opened it. And there, to his astonishment, stood a lovely young maiden.

"Forgive me for disturbing you, sir," she said. "But I seem to have lost my way . . ."

"Come inside, child. My goodness, you must

be freezing!" The old man asked his wife to prepare a bowl of hot rice gruel, and offered the girl a seat near the fire. "You'd better stay here tonight," he told her. "We've plenty of room."

"Oh, thank you, sir," said the girl. "You're very kind."

The old woman served the gruel and waited until the girl had eaten it before asking, "Where are you traveling to, miss?"

"Well . . ." The girl hesitated. "I haven't really decided yet."

A mere girl, traveling all alone with nowhere to go? She must have met with some great misfortune, thought the old man. He felt sorry for her and told her she was welcome to stay with him and his wife for as long as she liked. They'd be glad, he said, for the help and companionship.

"Do you really mean it?" cried the girl. "Oh, that would be wonderful! I'd like very much to stay with you."

"Well, then, it's settled," the old man said. "Now let's get some sleep. We can talk more in the morning."

The old couple slept very well indeed that night. They were still snoring softly when the girl got up, well before dawn, and went to the kitchen. She wanted to have breakfast ready for them when they awoke. But every barrel and cupboard she looked in was bare. There wasn't a grain of rice or a pinch of miso to be found.

What she did find, however, was a basket filled with spools of thread. She took this and disappeared into the workroom next to the kitchen, closing the door behind her. Soon from behind the closed door came the sound of a loom.

Creak, tap, clack . . . Creak, tap, clack . . . Creak, tap, clack . . .

The old man and woman awoke shortly after sunrise and saw that the girl wasn't in her bed. Before they even had a chance to wonder what had happened to her, however, she appeared in the doorway, carrying a thick roll of woven brocade.

"What beautiful cloth!" exclaimed the old man.

"Yes, it really is lovely," the old woman agreed. She took the brocade in her hands and marveled at its wonderful design.

"I made it for you," said the girl. "Please take it and sell it. Then buy some rice and miso, and anything else you might need."

The old man was delighted. He took the brocade to town that morning and sold it for a very good price. With the money he bought lots of food and a pretty comb for the girl. That night, after a delicious dinner, the three of them chatted contentedly by the fire.

"Well," said the old man when it had grown quite late, "why don't we turn in? We're sure to have sweet dreams tonight."

"Please go ahead," said the girl. "I have a bit more work to do."

"Oh no you don't. You've got to get your rest, child."

"I'm fine, really. I only want to weave a little more cloth for you." The girl looked down at her delicate white hands. "But I have a favor to ask. I want you to promise you'll never open the door to the workroom when I'm in there."

"Hm? You don't want us to see you weaving?"

"That's right. Please promise."

The old man and woman were puzzled by this odd request. But the girl was so insistent that finally they gave their word not to disturb her while she worked.

Each night from then on, the girl would weave a roll of beautiful brocade. And each day the old man would take the cloth to town and sell it at an excellent price. Soon there was enough rice and miso in the old couple's kitchen to last for months.

But with each passing day the girl grew paler and thinner. One evening the old man noticed her sitting by the open door, gazing wearily at the setting sun. She looked as if she might collapse at any moment. And later, at

dinner, she hardly touched her food at all.

"Eat, child. You've got to eat . . ."

"I've had enough, thank you. There's a little more work I want to do."

"You're overdoing it, dear," said the old woman. "You have to rest. It's not good for you to work so hard."

But the girl wouldn't listen. She stood up, swaying, to leave the table.

"Look how weak you've become!" cried the old man. He rose to stop her, but the girl shook her head and looked deep into his eyes.

"Just one more roll," she said, and walked unsteadily into the workroom, closing the door behind her.

That night, the old couple were so worried about the girl that they couldn't get to sleep.

"Dear," whispered the old woman. "Listen to the loom. It sounds . . . different tonight, somehow. I have a feeling something's very wrong."

The old man had the same feeling. "I'm going to have a look," he said, getting up.

"You can't do that, dear. You promised her . . ." But the old man was too concerned about the girl to let the promise stop him. He tiptoed to the workroom, opened the door a crack, and peered inside.

"Good heavens!" he gasped.

Sitting before the loom was a slender white crane. As the old man watched, the crane plucked one of its own feathers and carefully wove it into the cloth. Trembling, the bird was about to take hold of another feather when the old man flung open the door. The startled crane noticed him now for the first time and, right before his unbelieving eyes, slowly began transforming back into the lovely young maiden.

"You . . . You're . . ."

The girl hung her head and said, "Yes. I'm the crane you set free."

"Ah! That night in the marsh . . ."

"Yes. You saved my life. I wanted to repay you somehow. But now that you've discovered my secret . . ." The girl ran out of the workroom to the front door. "I must go. I wish I could stay forever, but . . ."

With a sad glance back at the old man, the girl dashed out across the yard. And as she ran, she turned once again into a beautiful white crane. Spreading her wings, she lifted off gracefully into the night sky.

"Remember us, child! Don't ever forget us!" the old man called after her. "We love you!" He reached for the comb he had bought the girl, ran outside, and threw it into the air.

The crane circled back, caught the comb in her beak, and uttered a sorrowful cry of parting. Then she rose higher in the sky and vanished amid the moonlit clouds.

NOTES

BABY GRANDMA（赤ん坊になったお婆さん）

p. 7　**3** way out in the country 草深いいなかに　　**5** feeble 弱い，かよわい　　**5** it was all they could do to make it through each day 一日一日を何とかやっていくのがやっとだった　　**8** managed somehow to get by なんとか暮していた　　**11** fireplace いろり　　**13** leak 雨もりがする　　**13** Plip. Plop. ポタン。ポトン。

p. 8　**2** I'd fix that leak if I could. できれば雨もりの穴をふさごうと思う。　　**3** I'm not as young as I used to be. 昔のように若くはない。　　**7** with each passing day 一日一日が過ぎるたびに　　**8** in turn 代わるがわる，順番に　　**8** dependent on〜 〜に頼って　　**14** gather firewood しばを刈る，たきぎを採る　　**15** spied some mushrooms きのこを見つけた　　**17** Long as I'm here, I might as well pick some for her. おそくなったが，ばあさまにきのこを採っていってやろう。　　**19** with his bundle of firewood strapped to his back しばの束を背負ったまま　　**20** shuffled along 足をひきずって歩いた

p. 9　**2** was lost 道に迷った　　**3** what's more そのうえ，おまけに　　**11** parting the bushes as he went しげみをかきわけて行くと　　**14** Thank goodness! ありがたや，よかった。　　**14** kneel down ひざまずく　　**16** nice and cold とても冷たい　　**17** scooped up a handful 手ですくった　　**18** delicious おいしい　　**19** took another sip もう一口飲んだ　　**20** sensed a rush of youthful energy 若々しい力がみなぎってくるのを感じた　　**23** reflection （水に映った）影　　**24** rippling pool さざなみの立つ水たまり　　**26** the wrinkles on his brow 額のしわ

p. 10　**2** shiny black 光るように黒い　　**6** full of pep and vitality 元気いっぱいで　　**6** was astonished by〜 〜に驚いた　　**8** that was nothing compared to〜 〜と比べれば何でもなかった　　**14** lost my way 道に迷った

p. 11　**1** cocked her head 首をかしげた　　**1** who might you be, young fellow どこの若い衆だろう　　**2** What can I do for you? 何のご用ですか。　　**6** nap 居眠りする　　**7** Rub the sleep out

111

of your eyes. 目をこすって眠気をはらえ。　**8** wide awake すっかり目が覚めて　**14** peer at～ ～をじっと見る　**23** turned this over in his mind このことをじっくり考えて

p. 12　**2** water barrel 水おけ　**12** the fountain of youth 若返りの泉　**13** with a crash どしんと　**18** all by myself 一人ぼっちで　**20** gourd ひょうたん　**24** that'll give us something to look forward to それを楽しみにしましょう

p. 13　**1** Heavens, no. ちっともかまいませんよ。　**2** patient 気が長い　**4** youthful 若々しい　**5** His snores echoed throughout the house. いびきが家中に響き渡った。　**8** couldn't sleep a wink 一睡もできなかった　**10** set off 出発する　**13** at dawn 夜あけに　**16** chuckled to himself ひとりでクスクス笑った　**23** bustled about tending to all the other chores 他の雑用を全部どしどし片付けた

p. 14　**1** the day wore on 時が経った　**1** there was no sign of～ ～の帰ってくる気配はなかった　**3** got lost 道に迷った　**5** convinced that～ ～を確信して　**7** as fast as his young legs would carry him 若い脚で走れるだけ速く　**10** sounds like a baby crying 赤ん坊の泣き声のようだ　**12** push on 急ぐ

p. 15　**1** Don't tell me she fell in! まさかばあさまが落ちたんではないだろうな。　**3** was about to pick it up 拾い上げようとした　**3** jumped back with a gasp あえぎながら跳びざさった　**10** It had turned her into an infant. ばあさまは赤ん坊になってしまった。　**14** they say ～だそうだ　**15** change diapers おむつをかえる　**16** clean up after～ ～を世話してきれいにする

HACHISUKE AND THE WHITE FOX
（はち助いなり）

p. 16　**2** the Lord of Obama 小浜の殿さま　**3** stroll through～ ～をみまわる，散歩する　**5** a fast-growing, bustling seaport 急成長のにぎやかな港町　**6** kindhearted 親切な，心の優しい　**7** took a leisurely walk のんびり散歩した　**8** mix with the local people 領民とまじわる　**9** on this particular day この日

に限って　　**9** he was making his way back to the castle when~ お城へ帰ろうとしていると~　　**12** came skidding around a corner 角を曲って横すべりして来た　　**17** thief どろぼう　　**17** yell 叫ぶ

p. 17　**1** pounce on~ ~に急にとびかかる　　**3** yelped and howled in pain 痛そうにキャンキャン泣きさけんだ　　**6** approach 近づく　　**9** your lordship 殿さま（呼びかけ）　　**12** chewed up our dried fish ひものをあらした　　**12** What a mess! しょうがないやつだ！　　**13** I'll tell you what. あのね（いい話がある）。　　**14** pay for the damage 損した分を償う　　**15** hand~over to… ~を…に手渡す　　**18** spare no expense in caring for~ 費用を惜しまないで~をかいほうする　　**20** fried tofu 油あげ　　**20** a great favorite of~ ~の大好物　　**21** treatment 手当て　　**22** in no time たちまち　　**23** as healthy and frisky as ever 前と同じように丈夫で元気な　　**25** had completely recovered 完全に直った

p. 18　**2** the foot of a mountain 山のふもと　　**6** let the fox go きつねを放した　　**12** trotted hesitantly up the moonlit mountain path 月明りの山道をためらいがちに走って行った　　**13** time and again 何度も何度も　　**16** mischievous いたずら好きな　　**18** prosper 栄える　　**19** fateful 宿命的な，重大な　　**21** see to it that a certain message was delivered to Edo ある手紙を江戸へ届けるようにする　　**24** be disgraced and ruined 家名を汚し破滅する

p. 19　**2** at his wit's end 思案に暮れて，途方にくれて　　**5** as a matter of fact 実際，実を言うと　　**10** bowed deeply and introduced himself 低くお辞儀をして自ら名乗った　　**13** if I can be of any assistance… 何かお手伝いができれば　　**18** sigh ため息をつく　　**20** hesitate ためらう

p. 20　**2** confident 自信に満ちて　　**3** slapping his knee ひざをたたいて　　**4** hire （人を）雇う　　**6** the box containing the vital letter 大事な手紙の入った箱　　**7** was off and running 走り出した　　**15** no sooner had he said this than~ こう言うか言わないうちに　　**18** buried his face in his hands 両手で顔をおおって　　**20** make it うまくやりとげる　　**20** it's all over now もうだめだ

22 misunderstand 誤解する

p. 21　**5** summon 召喚する，呼び出す　**5** fell to his knees ひざまずいた　**6** presented him with～ 殿さまに～を差出した　**7** was as delighted as he was flabbergasted びっくり仰天すると同時に喜んだ　**9** official 公式の　**11** repay～ ～に報いる　**12** be of service to～ ～のお役に立つ　**15** make it to Edo and back 江戸へ往復する

p. 22　**7** mission 役目，任務　**11** by the way ところで　**17** except for～ ～を除いて　**22** blushed and scratched his head in embarrassment 赤くなっててれくさそうに頭をかいた

p. 23　**6** well into the third week 三週目に入ってかなりたって　**7** get worried 心配になる　**9** with a shudder 身震いして，ぞっとして　**15** saddle some horses 馬に鞍を置く　**18** searched for several days with no luck 何日もさがしたが見つからなかった　**21** pointed at something in the weeds 草むらの中にあるものを指さした

p. 24　**1** a white object 白い物　**3** investigate 調べる　**6** Any trace of Hachisuke? はち助の手がかりがあったか？　**7** dismount（馬から）下りる　**8** turned ghostly pale まっ青になった　**11** limp くにゃくにゃした　**12** was draped over～ ～にもたれていた　**12** as if to protect it 箱を守ろうとするかのように

p. 25　**4** one and the same 全く同一の　**8** transformed himself into the fleet-footed messenger 足の速い飛脚に変身した　**10** tracked down and savagely attacked by～ ～に追い詰められ，ひどくおそわれて　**11** died of his wounds 傷がもとで死んだ　**12** struggled to make it back to～ なんとか～へたどり着こうとした　**15** shrine 神社，やしろ　**16** is named after～ ～の名をとって名付けた　**17** it's dedicated to Inari, the fox-deity いなり，つまりきつねの神さまを祭っている　**18** look out for～ ～の世話をする，面倒を見る

PRINCESS FLOWERPOT（鉢かつぎ姫）

p. 26　**4** sweet-natured 気立てのよい　**5** estate 地所

p. 27　**3** look after～ ～の世話をする　**5** Kannon, the Goddess of Mercy 慈悲の女神，観音さま　**7** pray 祈る　**7** what will become of～ ～はどうなるだろう　**10** well past midnight 最夜中をずっと過ぎて

p. 28　**3** flowerpot 鉢　**4** an unusual piece of advice 変わった忠告　**5** to say the least 控えめに言っても　**12** whispered weakly 弱々しい声でささやいた　**25** pull as he might どんなに引っぱっても

p. 29　**2** loosen ゆるめる，はずす　**4** that's the way it stayed そんな状態だった　**4** before long まもなく　**5** became used to～ ～に慣れてきた　**6** took to calling her "Flowerpot" 「鉢かつぎ姫」と呼ぶようになった　**7** bothered to～ わざわざ～した　**7** that is つまり　**13** scowl 顔をしかめる　**13** Disgusting little creature. きみの悪い子だわ。　**14** hiss シーと言う　**15** ridiculous こっけいな，ばかげた　**17** cold-hearted stepmother 冷淡な継母

p. 30　**1** despise 軽べつする　**2** freezing 凍るような　**3** get rid of the horrid little girl あのきみの悪い子を処分する　**8** a snowy wilderness 雪の野原　**10** wander through the countryside あちこちさまよい歩く　**10** penniless 無一文の　**11** having that pot stuck to her head didn't help 鉢が頭にぴったりくっついていることは役に立たなかった　**14** mean 意地の悪い　**15** tease いじめる

p. 31　**2** somehow or other ぜひなんとかして　**2** survive 生きながらえる　**4** wish she'd never been born 生まれなければよかったと思う　**6** pier 桟橋　**16** current 流れ　**18** was washed ashore 川岸に打ち上げられた　**18** exhausted くたくたになって

p. 32　**2** rescue 救う，助ける　**20** grew quite fond of～ ～がすっかり好きになった　**21** kept to herself 人づきあいを避けた　**24**

storeroom 物置　**24** came across an old thirteen-stringed koto 古い十三弦の琴を見つけた

p. 33　**2** pluck the strings quietly 静かに弦をかき鳴らす　**3** it so happened that～ たまたま～した　**12** I've always had a feeling about you あなたのことは気になっていました

p. 34　**2** touched his heart 彼の心をうった，感動させた　**9** arrange a splendid match すばらしいお嫁さんを決める　**13** overhear ふと耳にする　**14** rushed to Flowerpot's 鉢かつぎの部屋にかけつけた　**18** bride 花嫁

p. 35　**2** deep in thought 物思いにふけって　**4** Over my dead body! おれの死骸を乗り越えてやれ。→断じてゆるさぬ。　**15** upset 狼狽して，気も転倒して　**20** steal through～ ～をこっそり通る　**26** caught her by the hand 鉢かつぎの手を取った

p. 36　**3** I'd have no more of this nonsense! もうばかなまねはよせ！　**5** wench 娘，女　**5** have her head 首を取る，殺す　**9** Get out of the way! じゃまをするな！　**13** glow with a blinding, brilliant light 目をくらますような，けんらんたる光が輝く　**14** as if by magic まるで魔法のように　**15** shattered and fell to the ground in a million pieces こなごなにくだけて地面に散った　**17** stared in amazement 驚いて目をみはった　**19** budge （ちょっと）動かす

p. 37　**1** for the first time 初めて　**2** stammer どもりながら言う　**4** was stunned by Flowerpot's dazzling beauty 鉢かつぎのまぶしいような美しさに唖然とした　**5** I owe you an apology. おわびしなければならない。　**8** accept his offer of marriage 結婚の申し出を受ける　**10** ever after それからいつまでも　**10** come to think of it 考えてみると　**11** if it hadn't been for～ もし～がなかったら

THE SNOW WOMAN（雪女）

p. 38　3 woodcutter 木こり　9 trudge　through～ ～をとぼとぼ歩く　10 without spotting even so much as a rabbit うさぎさえも見つからずに　15 erasing the hunters' footprints behind them 歩くそばから足跡をかき消して

p. 39　6 stumble upon a woodcutter's hut きこり小屋を偶然見つける　12 stacked some wood in the fireplace いろりにたきぎをくべた　15 the flickering fire ちろちろと燃えるいろりの火　16 howl うなる，ヒューヒューいう　18 a good heart-to-heart talk 率直な話，腹蔵のない話　26 little did he know that～ ～を少しも知らなかった

p. 40　4 were fast asleep ぐっすり眠っていた　5 rage 猛威をふるう　6 an especially strong gust of wind とりわけ強い一陣の風　7 blew the door ajar 戸を少し開けた　7 came swirling into～ ～に舞いこんできた　8 put out the fire 火を消す　9 shiver 震える　17 dressed in flowing white silk 流れるような白い絹を着た　19 as pale and smooth as polished ivory みがいた象牙のように白くなめらかな　21 felt a shiver run down his spine 冷たいものが背筋を走るのを感じた，ぞっとした　23 ignore 無視する　26 exhaled a frosty white cloud 冷い白い息を吐きだした

p. 41　4 response 返答　7 blocking his path 行く手をさえぎって　9 to his horror and bewilderment ぞっとして当惑したことに　9 her cruel gaze softened 冷い目つきがやさしくなった　12 full of life 元気いっぱいで　18 buckle （ひざが）くずれる　19 unconscious 意識を失って

p. 42　4 frozen to death こごえ死んで　6 pay their respects 忌意を表する　7 comfort なぐさめる　7 blizzard 吹雪　15 shelter beneath the eaves of～ ～の軒下で雨やどりする　19 was on her way to～ ～へ行く途中だった

p. 43　4 almost before either of them realized it どちらからともなく　9 a match made in heaven すばらしい縁組み　10 were blessed with~ ～にめぐまれた　　**11** was a cheerful, devoted wife and mother 快活で献身的な妻であり母であった　　**15** delicate health 病弱　　**17** listless 大儀そうな，ものうげな　　**17** care for~ ～の世話をする，面倒をみる　　**18** the cool breezes of evening never failed to revive her 夕方の涼しい風が吹くとかならず元気を回復した　　**21** do her sewing 針仕事をする　　**25** for the thousandth time 何度となく

p. 44　　**4** profile 横顔　　**13** were caught in~ ～にあった　　**18** You had to say it, didn't you? それを言ってはいけなかったんじゃないの。　　**19** a harsh whisper きびしい小声

p. 45　　**5** legendary 伝説の　　**6** now that~ いまや～なので　　**7** she had no choice ほかに道はなかった　　**8** destroy 滅ぼす，殺す　　**9** bring herself to~ ～する気になる　　**18** Take care of yourself. からだに気をつけて下さい。

p. 46　　**5** was never to see~ ～を見ることはなかった　　**9** crying out in a chilling whine ひゅうひゅうと悲しく泣いて

TENGU'S VANISHING CLOAK（天狗のかくれみの）

p. 47　　**5** get into trouble 悶着を起こす　　**7** goblin 妖怪　　**7** the nearby mountain forest 近くの山の奥　　**9** cloak みの　　**10** invisible 目にみえない　　**12** get his hands on~ ～を手に入れる　　**15** hollowed out a piece of bamboo 一本の竹をくりぬいた

p. 48　　**3** peer through the bamboo tube 竹筒をのぞく　　**6** It wasn't long before he heard a rustling in the trees. まもなく木のざわつく音が聞えた。　　**8** smiled to himself 腹の中でにやりとした　　**11** raspy きしむような　　**12** pine tree 松の木　　**13** acted surprised 驚いたふりをした　　**17** No way!（それは）だめだ！いやだ！　　**19** spyglass 小型望遠鏡

p. 49　　**3** Tell you what. じゃ，こうしよう。　　**9** Come on さあさあ，早く早く。　　**10** pretend ふりをする　　**13** Now you are talking. そうこなくちゃ。そいつは話せる。　　**15** made the swap 交換をした

p. 50　　**1** was nowhere to be found どこにも見えなかった　　**3** scurry

down the mountain 山を急いで下る　　**4** play tricks on〜　〜に
いたずらをする　　**8** try it out on people 人々にためしてみる
13 load 荷物　　**14** trip ころばせる　　**15** he growled, picking
himself up off the ground 地面から起き上って怒って言った

p. 51　**1** shriek 金切り声を上げる　　**2** claim that〜　〜と主張する
3 pinch つねる　　**4** had her ears tweaked 耳を引っ張られた
4 let out a squeal 悲鳴をあげた　　**5** bald 禿げた　　**5** doze 居
眠りする　　**6** a big slap on the forehead 額をピシャリとたたか
れること　　**8** Fights started breaking out. ほうぼうでけんかが
始まった。　　**10** poked me in the eye わたしの目をつついた
12 octopus たこ　　**13** in midair 中空に　　**14** dumplings だん
ご　　**16** by itself ひとりでに　　**17** confusion 混乱，てんやわ
んや　　**19** have the time of his life 今までにないほどおもしろく
過ごす

p. 52　**1** head back to〜　〜へ戻る　　**4** I'm home. ただいま。いま帰っ
たで。　　**14** Something wrong with your eyes, Grandma? 目
が悪いんじゃないのかい，おばあ。

p. 53　**4** a pile of burning rubbish 燃えているゴミの山　　**5**
sleepyhead 寝坊助　　**14** filthy きたない　　**16** was crushed が
っくりした　　**17** precious 貴重な　　**17** go up in flames 燃え上
がる，消えてなくなる

p. 54　**1** sure enough はたして，案の定　　**3** genius 天才　　**8** came
screeching to a halt キキーと立止った　　**10** sweet bean-jam
buns 甘いあんこの入った丸パン（＝まんじゅう）　　**12** There
was nothing Hikohachi loved more than manju. まんじゅうは
彦八の大好物だった。　　**13** began gobbling them down one
after the other 次から次へとまんじゅうをばくばく食べ始めた

p. 55　**3** spooky 気味の悪い　　**5** broke out in a sweat どっと汗が出た
6 washed off the ashes in streaks 灰をおとして縞のようにした
7 little by little 少しずつ　　**12** There was nothing for him to
do but jump in. 川に跳び込むより仕方がなかった。　　**14**
Splash! ボチャン！

p. 56　**3** he came to wish he'd never heard of 〜 〜のことなど知らなけ
ればよかったと思うようになった

GRANDFATHER CHERRY BLOSSOM
（花咲か爺さん）

p. 57　**4** was plowing his field 畑をたがやしていた　**6** greedy old grouch よくばりの気むずかし屋の老人，よくばりじいさん　**9** Yip! Yip! Yip! キャン，キャン。　**9** puppy 子犬　**13** mutt 犬，のら犬　**13** tear up 荒らす　**16** whimper くんくん泣く　**16** he didn't mean any harm 畑を荒らすつもりはなかった　**17** overlook it just this once 今度だけは見のがす

p. 58　**3** I'll make sure he doesn't bother you any more. きっともう迷惑をかけないようにします。　**6** suit yourself 好きなようにしろ　**11** stray 迷い子の　**13** fresh-fallen snow 降ったばかりの雪　**14** appetite 食欲　**16** the more he ate the larger he grew 食べれば食べるほど大きくなった　**19** hoe 鍬を入れる　**20** tugged at his sleeve そでをくわえて引っぱった　**22** I'm kind of busy わしはちょっと忙がしいんだ　**23** leave him alone 放す

p. 59　**3** Arf, arf! ワンワン。　**5** shrug 肩をすくめる　**8** kneel down ひざまずく　**17** was green with envy ひどくねたんだ

p. 60　**6** mercilessly 冷酷に　**8** Shiro's strength gave out しろの力が尽きた　**8** he fell over, panting 息切れして倒れた　**12** clank! ガチッ！ガツン！　**13** Hooray! 万歳！　**16** slimy snakes ぬるぬるしたヘビ　**17** weird, smelly goblins 気味の悪いいやなにおいのする化けもの　**22** their fear gave way to rage 恐怖が怒りに代わった　**25** make a fool of ～ ～をばかにする

p. 61　**3** heartbroken 悲嘆に暮れた　**7** say a prayer お祈りをする　**11** wondrous 驚くべき，不思議な　**13** at an unbelievable speed 信じられないような速さで　**14** reach around it ひとかかえする

p. 62　**2** mortar うす　**6** shaped part of the trunk into～ 幹の一部を～にした　**7** pound mochi もちをつく　**14** Oomph! うん！　**16** wooden mallet 木の槌（つち）　**17** kneaded the gradual-

120

ly thickening dough だんだん腰が強くなってきたもちをこねた **18** sticky ねばねばした

p. 63 **2** rolled it into little round cakes 丸めて小さなもちにした **5** harden 堅くなる **16** stingy けちな, しみったれた **26** in a row 一列に

p. 64 **3** a mass of gooey black charcoal ねばねばした黒いすみのかたまり **4** stared at the mess in disgust うんざりしてそのきたない物を見つめた **6** Poof! プーッ！ **6** explode 爆発する, はねる **7** flames and black soot 炎と黒いすす **8** sputter ぶつぶつ言う **9** grabbed his axe 斧をつかんだ **9** chopped the mortar into tiny bits うすを小さく割った **12** broke down 気落ちした, がっかりした

p. 65 **4** scatter まきちらす **5** giant radish 大根 **11** withered 枯れた **15** sprang back to life 突然生きかえった

p. 66 **2** Goodness gracious! おやまあ, あら大変 **5** sprinkle まく **13** wildfire 野火, 燎原の火 **15** miracle 奇跡

p. 67 **7** if it please your lordship 殿様がお望みなら **8** come back to life and bloom 生き返って花が咲く **10** much to the daimyo's amazement その大名のとても驚いたことに

p. 68 **2** in the twinkling of an eye 瞬間に **5** Extraordinary! すばらしい！ **6** exclaim 叫ぶ **7** blossom-maker 花さかじじい **8** henceforth これからは **9** reward ほうびをとらせる

p. 69 **9** sneeze and cough くしゃみやせきをする **11** was enraged 怒った **11** Arrest that old impostor! あのかたり者のじじいをつかまえろ！ **15** it served him right いい気味だった

TANABATA（七夕さま）

p. 70 **3** the Milky Way 天の川 **3** mighty 巨大な, 広大な **4** on either side of its vast, raging current 広く荒れ狂う流れの両側に **5** Altair and Vega アルタイル（牽牛）とベガ（織女） **6** according to an old legend 古い伝説によれば **7** heavenly body 天体 **7** earthly 地上の, 下界の **11** star-crossed 星まわりの悪い, 幸（さち）薄い

p. 71　**8** robe 衣　**11** was delighted with his find 自分の見つけた物が気に入った　**12** worth a fortune 一財産の値打ちがある　**13** folded it up きちんとたたんだ　**21** celestial 天の　**25** her eyes brimming with tears 目は涙であふれんばかりにして　**26** belong on earth 下界の人間である

p. 72　**1** bathe 水浴びをする　**7** the moment he'd laid eyes on the heavenly maiden 天女を見たとたん　**12** pretended to search for～ ～をさがすふりをした　**14** Someone must have stolen it. だれかが盗んだにちがいない。　**22** as time went by 時がたつにつれて　**26** happy as she was with her earthly life 下界の生活に満足してはいたが

p. 73　**6** noticed her pet dove pecking at～ 鳩が～をつついているのに気づいた　**8** roofbeams 屋根の梁（はり）　**8** thrust its beak into～ ロばしを～につっこんだ　**16** garment 衣

p. 74　**4** weave a thousand pairs of straw sandals わらじを千足編む　**6** bamboo shoot たけのこ　**11** ascend 昇る　**15** be reunited with～ ～と再会する

p. 75　**3** at an incredible speed 信じられないような速さで　**4** in a matter of seconds 数秒のうちに　**5** tip 先端　**6** all I have to do is climb to the top てっぺんまで登っていきさえすればよい　**11** in his haste to～ ～するのを急ぐあまり、～したい一心で　**18** was working her loom 機（はた）を織っていた　**24** Hold on! 待って！　**26** grabbed hold of～ ～をつかんだ　**26** pulled himself up to～ ～へは上った

p. 76　**2** I missed you so much. さみしかったよ。　**5** a bearded and fearful-looking old man ひげをはやした恐ろしそうな老人　**7** roar わめく、どなる　**9** meekly おとなしく　**10** I'm honored to meet you. お目にかかれて光栄です。初めまして。　**13** a lowly earthling 卑しい下界の人間　**14** with a scowl こわい顔をして　**15** make your living 生計を立てる

p. 77　**3** seeds たね　**6** gulp ぐっとこらえる　**17** it would take years to～ ～するのに何年もかかるだろう　**22** replant まき直す　**24** dive and swoop and soar さっと舞い降りて舞い上がる

p. 78　**5** stand guard over the melon patch うり畑の番をする　**6** the Valley of Heaven 天の谷　**10** command 命令　**13** sacred

神聖な　　　16 swore 誓った　　　18 the scorching sun 焦げつくような太陽　　　18 his throat was so parched～ のどがかわいてしかたがなかったので　　　20 die of thirst のどの渇きで死ぬ　　　21 stand がまんする，たえる　　　22 ripe 熟れた　　　26 gush out of～ ～から噴き出る

p. 79　2 torrent 急流　　　3 was swept off his feet なぎ倒された　　　8 on opposite banks to～ ～の対岸に

BUNBUKU TEAKETTLE（分福茶釜）

p. 80　5 collect curios 古道具を集める　　　8 inspected his purchase 自分の買物をしげしげとながめた　　　9 sniffed at～ ～のにおいをかいだ　　　10 Sniff, sniff. くん，くん。　　　11 wrinkling his nose 鼻にしわを寄せて

p. 81　2 nice and shiny ピカピカな　　　3 grumble ブツブツ言う　　　5 complain 不平を言う　　　5 slap handfuls of wet sand on～ ～にたっぷり湿った砂を塗りつける　　　6 scrub away recklessly 乱暴にゴシゴシこする　　　20 do anything to get out of a little work 仕事をサボるためなら何でもする　　　22 be ashamed of yourselves 恥を知る　　　24 Enough of this nonsense! ばかなことはもうたくさんだ！　　　26 reluctantly いやいやながら，しぶしぶ

p. 82　1 rinsed the kettle out 茶釜を洗った　　　8 back away あとずさりする　　　12 come up with～ ～を考え出す　　　14 That'll be the day! まさか！　　　17 spurt out water 水を噴出する　　　23 want no part of～ ～なんて少しもほしくない　　　24 spooky 気味の悪い

p. 83　1 as luck would have it 運よく　　　1 tinker いかけ屋　　　8 for free ただで　　　11 humming contentedly 満足そうに鼻歌をうたいながら

p. 84　1 freshly caught fish 釣れたばかりの魚　　　3 grilled it over the fire 火で焼いた　　　7 the meal he had so looked forward to せっかく楽しみにしていた魚　　　9 was nowhere to be found 影も形もなかった　　　11 celebrate 祝う　　　13 on an empty stomach 空きっ腹で　　　21 sprout はやす，出す　　　26 frighten おどかす

p. 85 **1** plain 平凡な **5** You did give me quite a scare, you little rascal. こいつめ、まったくびっくりしたよ。 **14** can't afford to~ ~するゆとりがない **19** a turning-into-things-contest 「ばけくらべ」 **24** I'll put you up for tonight. 今夜はとめてやろう。

p. 86 **1** plead with~ ~に嘆願する **4** earn my keep 生活費をかせぐ **6** perform tricks 芸当をする ・**10** persuasive 説得力のある、口のうまい **12** public performance 公演、興行 **14** Come one, come all. さあ、らっしゃい、らっしゃい。 **15** tightrope-walker 綱渡り（師） **17** to the beat of~ ~の打つ音に合わせて

p. 87 **1** antics 芸当、道化 **2** become the talk of~ ~のうわさになる **3** from far and wide 四方八方から、各地から **4** pour in どんどん入る **5** live a life of luxury ぜいたくな暮しをする **6** owe it all to~ すべて~のお蔭である

p. 88 **13** collapsed with a dangerously high fever 高熱で倒れて重態になった **15** nurse him back to health 元気になるように看病する **16** cheer him up 元気づける **18** go see the cherry blossoms 花見に行く **25** he knew it was not to be そうはならないことは分っていた

p. 89 **5** had breathed his last 息を引取った

EARLESS HO-ICHI（耳なし芳一）

p. 90 **3** on the outskirts of~ ~のはずれに **4** Amida Temple 阿弥陀寺 **5** a musical monk named~ ~という琵琶弾き **8** lute リュート（弦楽器の一種） **10** a great master of the instrument 琵琶の名手 **12** perform the epic tale of the famous Heike clan 有名な平家の物語を演ずる **16** the great Battle of Dannoura 壇の浦の合戦

p. 91 **2** took place 行なわれた **3** the Straits of Shimonoseki 下関海峡 **7** feud 争い **9** ended with the defeat of~ ~の敗北で終った **11** among the victims was~ 犠牲者の中には~がいた **12** a tragic tale 悲劇 **13** no one could listen without

124

shedding a tear だれ一人なみだをさそわれぬものはなかった
15 humid むしむしする　**17** chant sutras お経を唱える

p. 92 **2** illustrious 高名な，著名な　**7** armour clanked and rattled
よろいがガシャガシャ音をたてた　**9** a dashing and noble
samurai 威勢のよい，りっぱな武士　**10** at length とうとう
11 spacious 広い　**11** an enormous banquet hall 大きな館
12 a great crowd of people 大勢の人々　**14** the rustle of silks
絹ずれの音　**14** the clatter of armor よろいのふれ合う音
19 as you wish, your ladyship かしこまりました，奥さま
24 the twanging bow strings ビュンという弓鳴りの音　**25** the
doomed warriors 不運の武者たち

p. 93 **1** faithfully 忠実に　**1** felt as if they were reliving that fateful
fight あの運命の合戦を再現しているような感じだった　**2** were
all deeply moved みな強く感動した　**3** muffled sobs むせび泣
きの声　**6** gentlewoman 女官，侍女　**8** express his appreciation 感謝を表わす　**14** be handsomely rewarded 何かふさわ
しいお礼をする　**15** mention 口に出す　**16** after solemnly
giving his word まじめに約束する　**17** took leave of the company 一行にいとまごいした　**17** was escorted back to～ ～へ
送られて戻った

p. 94 **9** suspicious 怪しいと思う　**9** keep an eye on～ ～から目を離
さないでいる，監視する　**11** a tremendous thunderstorm す
さまじい雷雨　**16** as instructed 指図されたように

p. 95 **5** were taking a shortcut through the cemetery 墓地の中の近道
を通っていた　**6** a great streak of lightning lit up the sky 稲光
が空を浮き上らせた　**13** dozens of phantom lights たくさんの
鬼火　**15** spirits 亡霊　**15** perish 滅びる　**19** with the
ghostly lights buzzing around them like angry bees 怒ったハチ
のように鬼火にまとわりつかれて　**24** was beside himself with
worry 心配で我を忘れた　**25** called for a brush and ink 筆と
墨を求めた　**26** Buddist sutras 経文

p. 96 **10** sit in meditation 座禅を組む　**10** don't move a muscle 身
じろぎひとつしない

p. 97 **1** looks like he left his ears behind あいつは耳だけ残していった
ようだ　**5** Rip! ビリッ！　**5** peeled them right off Ho-ichi's

125

head 芳一の頭から両の耳をはぎ取った　　6 terrible as the pain
was 痛みはひどかったが

p. 98　5 moan うめくように　　12 soul 人，人間

THE GRATITUDE OF THE CRANE （鶴の恩返し）

p. 99　6 get a bit lonely at times 時にはちょっと淋しくなる　　9 as
usual いつものように　　13 a frozen marsh 凍った沼　　16
with its leg caught in a hunter's trap 猟師のわなに足をかけられ
て

p. 100　2 set～free ～を放してやる　　2 flapped its wings つばさを羽ば
たいた　　8 chat idly のんびりおしゃべりする　　21 Forgive
me for disturbing you, sir. おじゃましてすみません。

p. 101　2 prepare a bowl of hot rice gruel 一杯のあたたかいおかゆを作っ
てあげる　　15 with nowhere to go 行くあてもなく　　17
must have met with some great misfortune 何か大きな不幸にあ
ったにちがいない　　23 companionship 交わり　　24 Do you
really mean it? 本当ですか。

p. 102　1 it's settled これで決った　　8 every barrel and cupboard she
looked in was bare 娘ののぞいた米びつや戸棚はどれも空っぱだ
った　　9 There wasn't grain of rice or a pinch of miso to be
found. 米ひとつぶ，みそひとつまみもなかった。　　13 spools
of thread 糸のたば　　14 workroom 機織り部屋　　18 creak,
tap, clack キー，トン，カラ

p. 103　3 a thick roll of woven brocade 厚い反物（たんもの）　　19
comb くし　　23 Why don't we turn in? もう寝ようかね。

p. 104　5 I have a favor to ask. お願いがあります。　　13 odd request
奇妙な頼み　　13 insistent しつこい　　21 last for months 何
か月ももつ　　25 wearily 疲れて　　25 She looked as if she
might collapse at any moment. 今にも倒れそうだった。

p. 105　5 You're overdoing it. お前は無理をしている。度が過ぎる。
9 swaying ふらふらして

p. 106　3 unsteadily よろよろと　　9 I have a feeling something's very
wrong. どこかおかしいような気がする。　　12 I'm going to go

have a look. ちょっと見てこよう。　　**17** was concerned about〜 〜のことが心配だった　　**18** tiptoe to〜 〜へ忍び足で歩く　　**22** slender ほっそりした

p. 107 **1** fling open〜 〜をガラッと開ける

p. 108 **4** lifted off gracefully into〜 ゆっくりと〜へ飛び立っていった　　**8** reach for〜 〜を取ろうと手を伸ばす　　**11** uttered a sorrowful cry of parting 悲しそうな別れの鳴き声をあげた　　**13** amid the moonlit clouds 月に照された雲の中に

（東京都立北多摩高等学校教諭　瀬戸武雄）

まんが日本昔ばなし 2
Once upon a Time in Japan 2

1986 年 12 月 10 日　第 1 刷発行
2005 年 11 月 29 日　第 28 刷発行

編　者　　川内彩友美

訳　者　　ラルフ・マッカーシー

発行者　　富田　充

発行所　　講談社インターナショナル株式会社

　　　　　〒 112-8652 東京都文京区音羽 1-17-14
　　　　　電話　03-3944-6493 （編集部）
　　　　　　　　03-3944-6492 （マーケティング部・業務部）
　　　　　ホームページ　www.kodansha-intl.com

印刷・製本所　大日本印刷株式会社